Little Pebble™

Little Creatures

Grasshoppers

by Lisa J. Amstutz

raintree

a Capstone company — publishers for children

Raintree is an imprint of Capstone Global Library Limited, a company incorporated in
England and Wales having its registered office at 264 Banbury Road, Oxford, OX2 7DY –
Registered company number: 6695582

www.raintree.co.uk
myorders@raintree.co.uk

Text © Capstone Global Library Limited 2018
The moral rights of the proprietor have been asserted.

Edited by Gena Chester
Designed by Sarah Bennet
Picture research by Wanda Winch
Production by Tori Abraham
Originated by Capstone Global Library Limited
Printed and bound in China

ISBN 978 1 4747 4777 6
21 20 19 18 17
10 9 8 7 6 5 4 3 2 1

British Library Cataloguing in Publication Data
A full catalogue record for this book is available from the British Library.

Acknowledgements
We would like to thank the following for permission to reproduce photographs: © Dwight
Kuhn - all Rights Reserved, 9; Dreamstime: Bevanward, 17; Minden Pictures: Stephen
Dalton, 5; Shutterstock: BestPhotoStudio, cover, blewulis, 7, boyphare, 11, Brian Maudsley,
21, Eric Isselee, 3, 24, evantravels, 1, Jaroslav Machacek, meadow background, Jordan Lye,
19, Jose Pinto, 13, Kirill Ilchenko, 15, Paul Reeves Photography, 22

Contents

Good jumpers

Hop! Hop!

A grasshopper jumps.

It has six legs.

It can jump far.

Grasshoppers are brown or green. They match dirt or grass. They hide from danger.

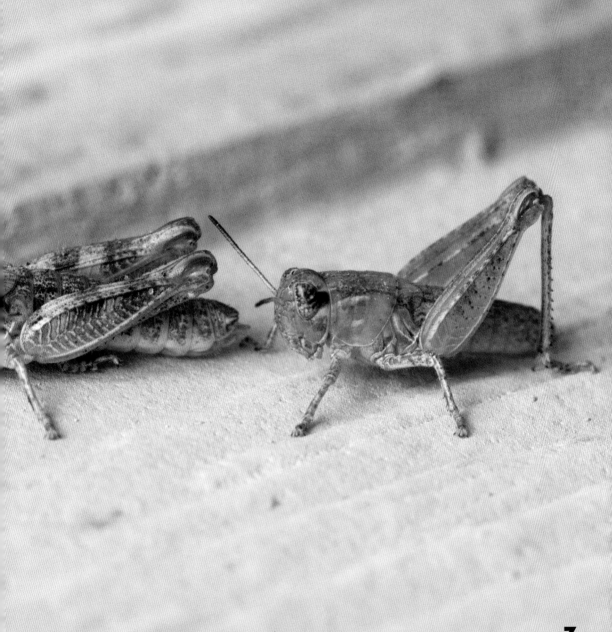

Look out!

A bird is near.

The grasshopper spits goo.

The bird takes off.

A grasshopper has

five eyes.

Two antennae smell food.

antennae

Time for lunch

Chomp!

Grasshoppers eat plants.

They eat bugs too.

Some grasshoppers form swarms. They eat and eat. They harm crops.

Growing up

A female digs a hole.

She lays eggs in it.

Babies hatch out.

Babies do not have wings.

They eat grass.

They shed their skin.

18

Wings grow.

It is time to fly.

Goodbye!

Glossary

antennae feelers on an insect's head used to sense smells and touch

crop plant farmers grow in large amounts, usually for food

match to be the same

spit force something out of the mouth; grasshoppers can spit brown goo at predators

swarm gather or fly close together in a large group

Find out more

Beastly Bugs (It's All About), (Kingfisher, 2016)

First Facts Bugs, (Dorling Kindersley, 2011)

Minibeast Body Parts (Animal Body Parts), Clare Lewis (Raintree, 2013)

Websites

www.bbc.co.uk/education/topics/z2p3kqt/resources/1
This BBC website has lots of clips about insects.

www.bugfacts.net/grasshopper.php
Visit this website to find information about grasshoppers, including where they live, what they eat and what they look like.

Critical thinking questions

1. How are grasshoppers harmful?
2. How do grasshoppers stay safe from birds?
3. Name two kinds of food that grasshoppers eat.

Index